LARK
CRAFTS

Published by Lark Crafts
An Imprint of Sterling Publishing Co., Inc.
387 Park Avenue South, New York, NY 10016

ISBN 978-1-4547-0020-3

This material originally appeared as part of
A Is for Apron (ISBN 9781600592010). First
publication in this format 2011.

© 2008, Lark Crafts

Distributed in Canada by Sterling Publishing,
c/o Canadian Manda Group, 165 Dufferin
Street, Toronto, Ontario, Canada M6K 3H6

Distributed in the United Kingdom by GMC
Distribution Services, Castle Place, 166 High
Street, Lewes, East Sussex, England BN7 1XU

Distributed in Australia by Capricorn Link
(Australia) Pty Ltd., P.O. Box 704, Windsor,
NSW 2756 Australia

Manufactured in China

contents

the Aprons

Apron Kit

You only need a few basic tools to make aprons, and even if you're a novice sewer, you probably already own almost of them.

Shears Typically a bit larger than scissors, high-quality dressmaker's shears have razor-sharp edges and a heft that makes cutting fabric a breeze. Never cut anything but fabric with them. Ever.

Scissors Keep a couple pairs on hand, one for trimming fabric and thread and—since paper dulls blades—a cheap pair for cutting out patterns and anything besides cloth.

Thread, pins, and needles For professional results, don't scrimp on quality with these, especially if you're working with delicate fabric.

Tape measure For accuracy, use one that doesn't stretch.

Sewing machine It's fine if your sewing machine makes nothing but straight stitches and zigzag, but machines with fancy embroidery stitches give you extra options for embellishments.

Iron and ironing board Use a sturdy padded ironing board and a steam iron.

Water-soluble fabric pens These pens make blue lines that disappear when you mist or dab them with water. Don't iron over them first or they could become permanent.

Transfer pencils Some sewers use transfer pencils to trace an embroidery design onto paper and then hot iron the design directly onto fabric. If you're low tech, however, you can always use the window method (page 8).

Techniques

aprons are pretty simple to make and perfect projects for a new sewer. Do note, if you don't already know how to sew, this book will not teach you how. You should already be aware of fabric grain and know how to lay out patterns, cut out fabric pieces, operate a sewing machine, and understand basic sewing terminology such as "topstitch" and "seam allowance."

Enlarging the Templates

You can enlarge the templates in the back of this book using a photocopier. If you're like me—too busy and (I'll be honest here) mathematically challenged—go to a place that offers large-format copying or take the book to a business that provides reprographic services, which means they print blueprints. It's so much simpler for the staff to scan the patterns, enlarge them in a few easy keystrokes, and print them on large sheets. Full-service copy shops can usually enlarge the templates for you, too; take that route if you don't mind taping several sheets of paper together.

Seam Allowances

Unless it's noted otherwise, the aprons in this book have seam allowances of ½ inch (1.3 cm).

Finishing Seams

If you wear your apron for more than show, it's going to go through a lot of washing and drying. This causes raw fabric edges to unravel, so finish all exposed seams or you'll end up with an ugly, frayed mess. Your choices for finishing include pinking, zigzagging, serging (if you've got a machine), or even la-de-da fancy French seams. Sure, it takes a little extra time, and it feels like a drag when you're in a hurry to get to the good part—the sewing. Hey, if you're okay with dangling dreadlocks of matted thread, you can skip this step.

Pressing

When sewing, you should press rather than iron. In pressing, you place the iron where you want it, give a little blast of steam to open up seams, then lift the iron and set it down again in a new area. In contrast, when ironing, the iron gets pulled across the fabric to smooth out wrinkles; this can stretch the fabric, and you don't want that. After pressing, pause a few seconds to let the piece cool before picking it up so the fabric doesn't stretch.

Pleating the Ties

You can create wide apron ties and then pleat them at the point where they attach to the waistband or apron front. Fold the fabric into one or two pleats—whatever you like—pin, then baste, making sure the basting stitches are parallel to the raw edge (figure 1). Press to flatten and make it easier to stitch it to the waistband.

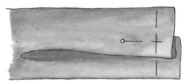

figure 1

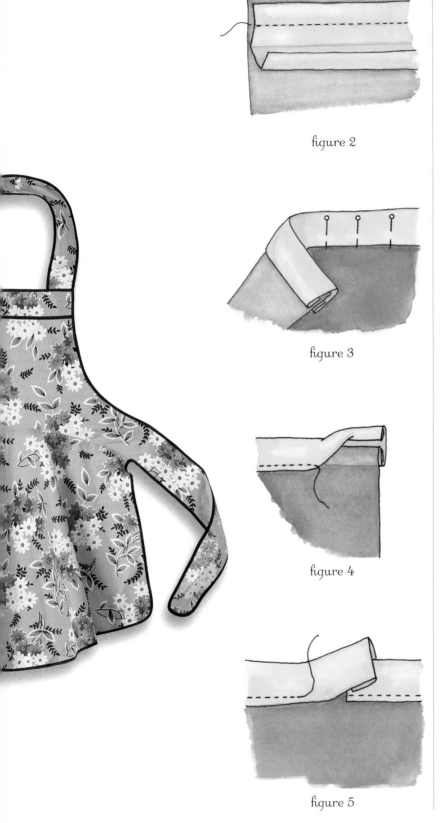

figure 2

figure 3

figure 4

figure 5

In a Bind: Sewing on Bias Tape

About a third of the aprons in this book are edged with bias binding. Here's how to apply either pre-packaged double-fold bias tape or bias strips you've made yourself (page 5). *Note:* The difference between ¼-inch (6 mm) double-fold bias tape and ½-inch (1.3 cm) single-fold is a pressing matter, literally. If you purchased single-fold bias tape, fold the strip in half lengthwise and press it to get ¼ inch (6 mm) double-fold tape, which is the width I recommend you use to bind an apron. (To make it clearer what's going on, all the illustrations except figure 5 show the binding beginning at the corner of the fabric, but when lapping ends, you should not start at a corner.)

1. Begin by sewing a row of stay-stitching ¾ inch (1.9 cm) away from all the raw edges to bind. Trim back the seam allowance so that only ⅛ inch (3 mm) remains beyond the line of stay stitching.

2. Measure the distance to bind, add 5 inches (12.7 cm), and cut this length of binding strip. With the folds in the tape facing away from the apron, pin one raw edge of the binding to the raw edge of the wrong side of the apron. Stitch around the edge in the crease of the tape (figure 2). Stop stitching 3 inches (7.6 cm) from the starting point and clip the loose end so that 1 inch (2.5 cm) of tape overlaps the part that's sewed down.

3. Flip the bias tape to the right side of the apron, fold the raw edge of the tape under, and pin it down, as shown in figure 3. Machine stitch near the fold of the bias tape (figure 4), stopping 2 inches (5.1 cm) from the starting point.

4. To tidy up the ends, lap them by folding the loose tail under ½ inch (1.3 cm), as shown in figure 5. Finish stitching the binding down.

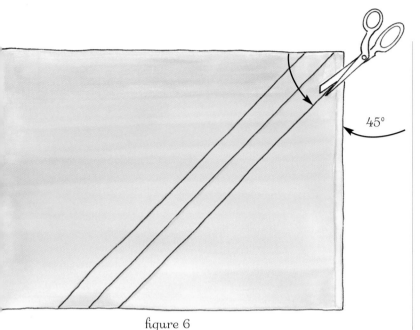

figure 6

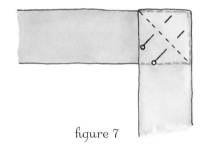

figure 7

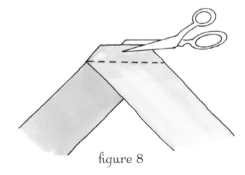

figure 8

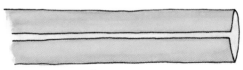

figure 9

Making Cool Bias Tape

Purchased bias tape is like a TV dinner—cheap and convenient, but ultimately kind of bland. Add spice by making your own bias tape. To give the appearance of perfect harmony with the apron's personality, use the same fabric as for the apron or a solid color that's a flawless match rather than a close one. To really pump up the flavor, cut bias tape from a complementary print. It only takes a few minutes and makes an apron really pop.

1. Cut strips four times as wide as your desired tape at lines running 45° to the selvage (figure 6). You'll need enough strips to create a band that, once stitched together, can cover the circumference of the apron plus some extra.

2. Place one strip over another at a right angle with the right sides together. Stitch diagonally from one corner to the next of the overlapping squares (figure 7).

3. Snip off the corners along the seam, leaving a ¼-inch (6 mm) seam allowance (figure 8). Open up the seams, and press the allowances flat. Repeat steps 2 and 3 with all the strips to make one long piece.

4. Fold the strip in half lengthwise, right side out, and press. Open the strip, and press the raw edges into the center. Now you have single-fold bias tape (figure 9).

To make double-fold bias tape, fold again in the center and press, as shown in figure 10.

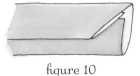

figure 10

Inserting Rickrack in Seams

Add a splash of fun to pockets or to lines of stitching by sewing rickrack into the seams.

1. Position the rickrack on the right side of the fabric so the "humps" along one side are parallel with and close to the raw edge. Pin the rickrack to keep it in place. Baste along the center of the rickrack using big stitches (figure 11).

2. Measure the distance between the edge of the fabric and the center line of the rickrack; this will be the seam allowance. Pin the piece of fabric and the element you wish to stitch it to, right sides together, and sew, using the determined seam allowance. When you turn the pieces right side out, you'll find the rickrack, sandwiched between, with only half of the humps showing.

figure 11

fit to be tied

One size fits most with the aprons in this book, but if you're concerned, you can make a muslin sample first. Obviously, you can easily alter aprons made of rectangular pieces (such as the one on page 36) by simply extending or reducing the width. Other aprons in this book can be slightly adjusted by altering the percentage by which you enlarge the templates. Other than this, it can be fairly complex to alter size considerably. While the front may fit, for example, the neck ties may not end up in the right place. If you're confident you know how to alter, have at it. Otherwise, leave it to a pro.

Flouncing Around: Making Ruffles

Need cheap frills? Gather 'round and learn how to make a ruffle.

1. Determine the depth of the ruffle and cut fabric strips at least two and a half times longer than the edge it will embellish.

2. Zigzag the raw edges to prevent fraying. Sew a narrow hem along one edge, lengthwise.

3. Sew two rows of basting stitches along the edge opposite the hem. Don't trim the thread ends; instead, pull them to gather the ruffle to the length and frilliness you want (figure 12).

4. Pin the ruffle to its base, right sides together, adjust the length and the gathers, and stitch. Et voilà!

figure 12

Hems

To create a simple ¼-inch (6 mm) hem, turn the fabric under ½ inch (1.3 cm) and press. Fold this under again by half, ending up with a double fold that's ¼ inch (6 mm) wide. Topstitch the hem on a machine, or hand-sew from the back.

Mitering Corners

Mitered corners are one of the classiest finishing techniques. The good news is they're nowhere near as difficult to make as they appear when finished. Mitering eliminates bulk and creates a tidy-looking 45° seam at the corners.

1. Press under the desired hem on each edge and then open out the folds. If you've made a double hem, open only one fold, not both. Fold the corner diagonally down to the place where the two fold lines intersect, as shown in figure 13. Note how the previous fold lines line up.

2. Press across the corner fold and check to see if you got it right by folding again along the original hemline. Your edges should now meet at a perfect angle. Cool, huh? Now unfold again and trim away excess fabric in the corner (figure 14).

3. Fold back into the mitered edge (figure 15) and slipstitch the mitered edges—the angle—together. Victory dance!

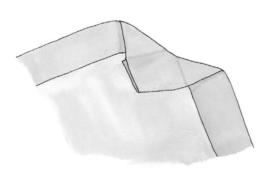

figure 13

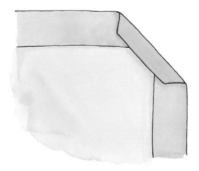

figure 14

figure 15

Stuck on Appliqué

An appliqué is a decorative piece of fabric applied to a base cloth. By now, you've noticed the high esteem in which I hold anything decorative; true to form, I love adding appliqués as an additional level of embellishment. You can leave the edges of an appliqué raw, or turn them under.

To camouflage the stitches attaching an appliqué, poke the needle through the base fabric and up through the appliqué, right next to the fold of the turned-under edge of the fabric. Bring the needle back down into the base fabric just a wee bit away. Repeat, as shown in figure 16. When the piece is completely sewn down, take a few tiny back stitches, work the needle under the appliqué piece and across to the other side, cut close to the edge, and pull slightly. The end of the thread will disappear under the appliqué piece.

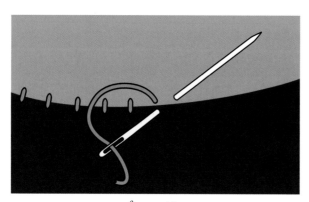

figure 16

Embroidery Primer

You can use as few as one or as many as six strands of floss in your needle, depending on how fine or broad you want a design to look. You don't have to be a stickler about using embroidery needles—just pick the smallest size and type you happen to have around that holds the desired amount of floss. On the other hand, always stretch the fabric in an embroidery hoop; stitching on floppy fabric is murder.

For a beginner, it's probably easier to transfer a ready-made design to follow the lines and fill in the spaces, but confident embroiderers can do free-form stitching.

Transferring Designs

The low-tech method for getting a printed image onto fabric involves taping the paper on a sunny window, putting the fabric over it, and tracing the design with a water-soluble marker. That's it, no additional widgets required. Can't do without gadgets? A transfer pencil is a nifty tool for transforming any image into a pattern to embroider. You'll also need tracing paper, an iron, and an ironing board.

1. Select the design to embroider. Put the tracing paper over it, and trace firmly using the transfer pencil. Note: If you have words, numbers, or anything that will read backwards when flipped, *reverse* that part of the design before tracing it. You only have to forget this once, and you'll never do it wrong again!

2. Flip the tracing paper over, image side down on the fabric. Pin it to the cloth so it doesn't shift, and press the tracing paper with a dry iron. Presto! The image is now on the cloth. Place it in a hoop and stitch away.

Designer Joan Hand Stroh

amoeba

Materials

Apron kit (page 2)

Pattern (page 51)

1 yard (91.4 cm) of fabric

6 yards (5.5 m) of ¼-inch
(6 mm) double-fold bias tape

Tool

Seam leveler

I prefer classic, tailored clothing, so I seldom make frilly aprons. Never underestimate the impact of a simple design.

—Joan Hand Stroh

What You Do

1 Make a true bias fold of the fabric (figure 1). Then cut out the apron using the pattern pieces on page 51. Transfer the dots from the front pattern piece onto the fabric. Don't stretch or pull the edges. Set the pieces aside.

2 Splice together the bias tape to create one long piece.

3 Bind the top edge of the apron front. Trim the binding ends even with the side edges.

4 Baste the bias tape to the ties, positioning carefully around the scallops. Press them down then sew them together, using the seam leveler if necessary. Trim the binding ends evenly across the ties.

5 Position one tie on the back side of the apron front, with the long end of the tie toward the top of the front (figure 2). Stitch close to the edge to hold the tie in place. Repeat to attach the other tie.

6 Bind the remainder of the apron front. Start on the right side, leaving about 1½ inches (3.8 cm) of binding free. Encase the edges, including the ties. Stitch around the sides and bottom of the front, mitering the corners and creating a small tuck at the bottom center of the front piece. Stitch off the end of the binding for about 1½ inches (3.8 cm).

7 Press the ties flat over the bias tape. Trim the binding end 1 inch (2.5 cm) from the top of the apron front. Fold the end under, placing it between the tie and the binding. Stitch through all thicknesses along the original stitching line.

8 Bind the top of the pocket. Trim the binding ends even with the pocket sides. Position the pocket on the skirt, matching the corners to the

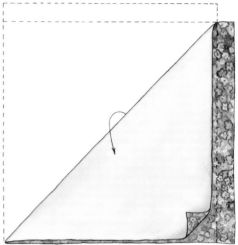

figure 1

dots, and pin it in place. Fold ⅜ inch (1 cm) of the bias tape under the top right corner. Stitch the pocket in place using the seam leveler at the corners if necessary. Stop with the needle down about 2 inches (5.1 cm) away from the left pocket corner. Trim the binding to about ⅜ inch (1 cm) from the top of the pocket and finish stitching. While wearing this apron, try to be modest about all the compliments!

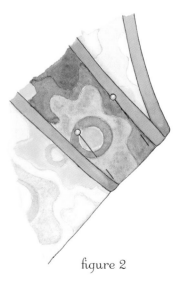

figure 2

Cakeland

Materials

Apron kit (page 2)

Pattern (page 52)

¾ yard (68.6 cm) of fabric for the overlayer

1 yard (91.4 cm) of fabric for the underlayer

¼ yard (22.9 cm) of fabric for the waistband

⅛ yard (11.4 cm) of fabric for the pocket

¼ yard (22.9 cm) of interfacing

3 yards (2.7 m) of rickrack

2½ yards (2.2 m) of ball fringe

1⅝ yards (1.5 m) of 4-inch-wide (10.2 cm) ribbon

What You Do

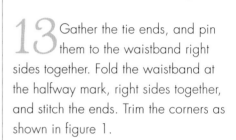

1 Enlarge and cut out the pattern pieces (page 52), lay them on the fabric, and transfer any placement marks. Cut them all out.

2 Using the appropriate pattern pieces, cut out interfacing for the waistband and the pocket.

3 Fuse the interfacing to the wrong side of the waistband and the pocket top edge.

4 Fold the top of the pocket over the interfacing and press. Pin the rickrack to the right side of the fabric around three sides of the pocket so that the middle of the rickrack is ¼ inch (6 mm) from the edge. Fold the rickrack to the outside, and sew it down with a ¼-inch (6 mm) seam allowance.

5 Stitch the width of the finished pocket top along both sides. Trim the corners and any extending rickrack, and then turn the pocket over to the wrong side. Fold the seam allowance along the stitching and press. When you turn the pocket to the right side, you should see the rickrack peeking from the edges. Set the pocket aside.

6 Using the overlayer, pin the top of the ball fringe to the outer edge of the right side of the fabric,

and sew it down. Fold the seam allowance to the wrong side of the fabric and press. Topstitch along the seam edge you created.

7 Place the completed pocket on the indicated spot on the overlayer, and stitch it down close to the edge.

8 At the waist of the overlayer, sew gathering stitches ¼ inch (6 mm) and ⅛ inch (3 mm) from the edge, and gather evenly, using the waistband as a guide for sizing. Set the overlayer aside.

9 Follow the instructions from step 4 to attach rickrack to the underlayer. Fold the seam allowance to the wrong side of the fabric and press. Topstitch close to the edge. Then repeat step 8 for the underlayer.

10 Place the underlayer right side up on a flat surface. Place the overlayer on top, matching the waistbands. Adjust the gathers so that 1 inch (2.5 cm) of the underlayer extends out from each edge of the overlayer.

11 Pin the waistband to the two layers right sides together. Stitch them together, and then press the seam allowances toward the waistband.

12 To construct ties from the ribbon, cut two lengths 28 inches (71.1 cm) long. Fold in ½ inch (1.3 cm) from one edge, and sew it down to create a hem.

13 Gather the tie ends, and pin them to the waistband right sides together. Fold the waistband at the halfway mark, right sides together, and stitch the ends. Trim the corners as shown in figure 1.

14 Turn the ends of the waistband right side out. On the wrong side of the apron, fold the raw edge of the waistband under, and pin it over the seam, covering the stitches. On the right side, stitch close to all edges of the waistband. Cupcake, anyone?

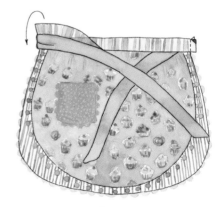

figure 1

cherry bistro

Materials

Apron kit (page 2)

Pattern (page 53)

1¼ yards (1.1 m) of cotton/
cotton blend fabric for the
apron front

⅓ yard (30.5 cm) of contrasting
fabric for the front panel

44 inches (1.1 m)
of jumbo rickrack

44 inches (1.1 m)
of medium rickrack

What You Do

1 Enlarge the pattern pieces on page 53, and cut them out of fabric.

2 To make the front panel, pin the jumbo rickrack to the contrasting fabric, 1¼ inches (3.2 cm) from each long edge. Sew two rows of stitching ¼ inch (6 mm) apart down the center of each rickrack column, removing the pins as you go. Center the medium rickrack over the jumbo, pin it, and sew.

3 Create tucks on the front panel piece by folding on the dotted line. Pin the tucks in place then baste a ⅜-inch (1 cm) seam from the top edge. Fold the rickrack over the bottom edge of the panel. Finish the outer edges and bottom with a ⅝-inch (1.6 cm) narrow hem.

4 To finish the apron front, sew a ⅝-inch (1.6 cm) narrow hem along the outer edges. Then machine stitch a 2-inch (5.1 cm) hem.

5 To make the ties, fold the fabric lengthwise in half, right sides together. Stitch one end and along the length of the tie, leaving one end open to turn it out. Trim the inside corners. Turn the tie right side out and press. Repeat to make the other tie.

"For me, the fun starts with the fabric. I come up with different color combinations and embellishments before thinking up the actual design."
—**Morgan Moore**

6 Center the finished front panel on the front of the apron, and baste stitch the pieces together at the top.

7 Fold in a ⅝-inch (1.6 cm) seam allowance on both edges of the waistband. Stitch the waistband to the apron front and front panel, right sides together, ensuring that the panel is securely in the seam. Fold the waistband over, inserting the open ends of each tie (figure 1). Topstitch the ties in place and along the edge of the waistband, catching the side underneath.

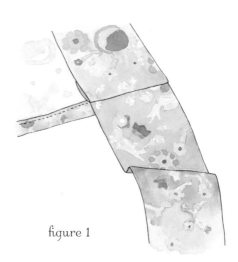

figure 1

lemon meringue

Materials

Apron kit (page 2)

Pattern (page 54)

½ yard (45.7 cm) of fabric
for the front

¼ yard (22.9 cm) of fabric
for the pockets

¼ yard (22.9 cm) of fabric
for the waistband and ties

1 package of rickrack

Interfacing

1 package of bias tape

Seam allowance:
¼ inch (6 mm)
unless otherwise noted

What You Do

1 Cut out all the apron pieces according to the pattern (page 54).

2 Finish the outer edges of the front of the apron, so they won't unravel. On the right side of the fabric, place the rickrack along the outer edges with its centerline ¼ inch (6 mm) from the edge. Stitch the rickrack down the center. Fold the fabric and the rickrack under along the stitch line and press. Turn and topstitch along the fold as close to the fold line as possible.

3 As in step 2, finish the outer and inner edges of the pocket, and then attach the rickrack to the right side. Fold the fabric and the rickrack under along the stitch line and press. Turn and topstitch the inner edge of the pocket. Repeat to make a second pocket.

4 Pin the pockets, right sides up, to the right side of the apron front, aligning the notches. Stitch across the top of the pocket and around the sides, close to the rickrack.

5 Fuse the interfacing to the wrong side of the waistband. With wrong sides together, fold the waistband lengthwise down the center and press.

" *When I first began sewing, I made aprons because there were no sleeves or zippers to fuss with, and the result always fit. But it's astonishing how many techniques I've learned specifically from aprons.* "

—Betsy Couzins

6 Pin the waistband to the top of the apron with right sides together, making sure the waistband extends ¼ inch (6 mm) beyond either side (figure 1, next page). Stitch, then press the seam allowances toward the waistband.

7 To create the tie, fold under the long side twice to make a ⅜-inch (1 cm) double hem. Press and stitch. To make a point, fold one end of the tie diagonally with right sides together, and then stitch it down along the long side, ⅜ inch (1 cm) from the edge. Turn the corner right side out, press, and then stitch the remaining long edge of the tie with a ⅜-inch (1 cm) double hem. Topstitch the point. Finally, create a pleat in the raw end of the tie that attaches to the apron (page 3). Repeat for the other tie.

8 With right sides together, pin the ties to the waistband, aligning the ties with the waist seam. Using the center line as a guide, fold the waistband over the ties. Stitch the ends to secure the ties (figure 2) then turn the waistband right side out.

9 On the wrong side of the front, fold the raw edge of the waistband under, and pin it over the waist seam. On the apron front, topstitch along the edges of the waistband.

figure 1

figure 2

fruit tart

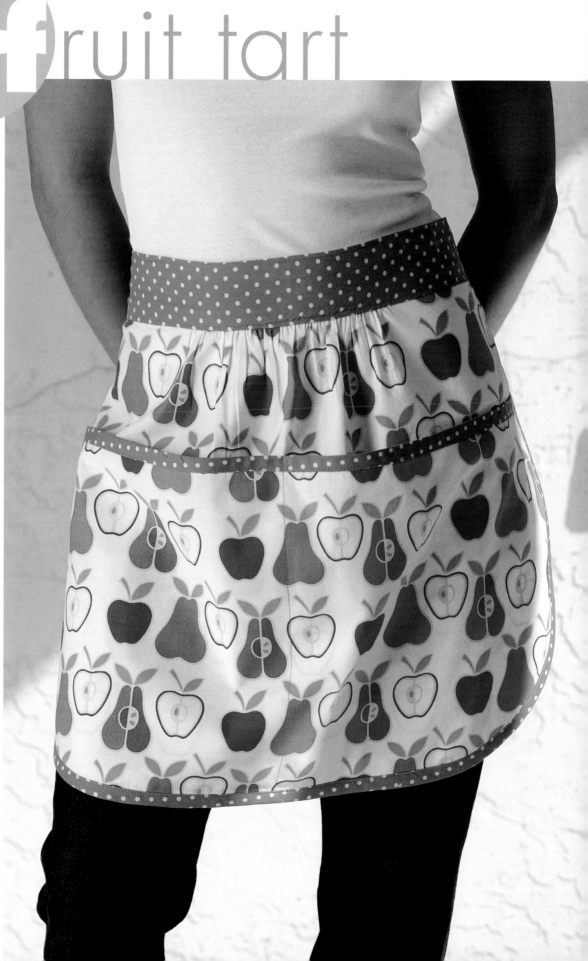

Materials

Apron kit (page 2)

Pattern (page 55)

⅞ yard (80 cm) of main fabric

¾ yard (68.6 cm) of coordinating fabric to make bias tape

" Even taking time out to experiment,
I can whip up an apron
in one afternoon,
start to finish. I love it! "
—**Nathalie Mornu**

What You Do

1 Enlarge the pattern pieces on page 55, and cut them out of fabric.

2 Make 7 feet (2.1 m) of bias tape 2 inches (5.1 cm) wide out of the coordinating fabric (page 5).

3 Stitch the bias tape to the top edge of the pocket pattern piece.

4 Pin the wrong side of the pocket to the right side of the front, matching the bottom edges. Baste ⅛ inch (3 mm) from the bottom edge.

5 Using a water-soluble marking pen, draw a vertical line at the center of the pocket, from top to bottom. Stitch along this line to split the pocket in half, reinforcing the stitching at the top by sewing back and forth a few times.

6 Stitch bias tape around the bottom edge of the front piece, including the pocket where it's basted on.

7 Gather the top of the front evenly between the notches. Set it aside.

8 Pin two of the ties with right sides together, matching all edges. Using a ⅜-inch (1 cm) seam allowance, stitch the edges, leaving the end with the squared corners open. Trim both of the angled corners, press the seams open, and turn right side out. Press flat, and topstitch ⅛ inch (3 mm) in from the edges. Pin and baste one pleat in the center of the open end (page 3). Repeat with the remaining pieces to make the other tie.

9 Put one waistband face up on your work surface. Pin the pleated end of a tie at the center of one side, with the tie placed across the band rather than on the outside of the band (figure 1). Repeat on the other side of the waistband.

figure 1

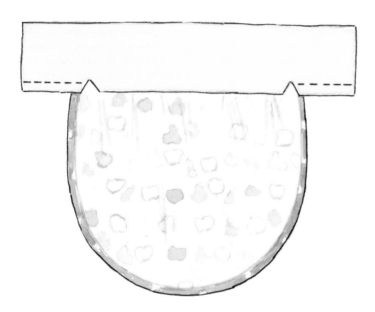

figure 2

10 Place the other waistband piece face down over the piece used in step 9, matching notches. Pin and sew the top and side edges, leaving the bottom notched edge unstitched. Clip the corners, and turn right side out.

11 Pin the apron front to the waistband, matching the notches, and baste. Turn the waistband inside out again. On the notched edge, stitch from each corner to the bias tape nearest it, making certain not to catch the tie ends in the seam (figure 2). Clip the corners.

12 Turn the waistband right side out and press. Topstitch the waistband closed ⅛ inch (3 mm) from the edge. Continue to topstitch around the entire waistband. Tie it on, and bake something sweet and gooey.

deep pockets

Materials

Apron kit (page 2)

Pattern (page 56)

⅝ yard (57.2 cm) of patterned fabric for the pocket

⅝ yard (57.2 cm) of solid fabric for the front

½ yard (45.7 cm) of fabric for the sash

38 inches (96.5 cm) of bias tape

What You Do

1 Cut one of each piece using the pattern pieces on page 56. Transfer the reverse of the fabric using tailor's chalk or a soft pencil.

2 Cut 5 inches (12.7 cm) of the bias tape, and fold it in half lengthwise. Press it. Stitch it to one corner of the front piece where marked on the pattern (figure 1). Repeat on the other corner.

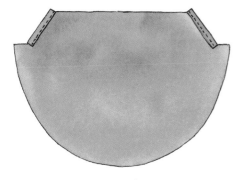

figure 1

3 Sew the bias tape to the upper curved edges of the pocket piece. To make this easier, first set a curve into the tape. Fold a 14-inch (35.6 cm) length in half lengthwise, and using an iron, curve it to the shape of the pocket, using the pattern as a guide. Pin it in place, and sew through all layers. Repeat for the second curve.

> *I enjoy using historical techniques and playing with shape, proportion, and structure. I let the nature of the fabric lead the design.*
>
> **—Ruth Singer**

4 Lay the two pieces right sides together with the front piece on top. Stitch around the bottom curved edge, using a ⅝-inch (1.6 cm) seam allowance. Finish the raw edges if desired. Notch the curved seams to help it lie flat, but don't cut the notches too close to the stitching.

5 Turn the apron right side out, and press it down, making sure the curved seam is turned out fully. Pin the top center of the pocket carefully in place so that it matches the top of the front. Stitch down the middle of the apron to make two pockets.

6 Make the sash by cutting a rectangle 7 x 70 inches (17.8 x 177.8 cm). Fold the fabric in half lengthwise, right sides together. Cut each end at an angle. With a ½-inch (1.3 cm) seam allowance, sew up one short end and 27 inches (68.6 cm) along the long edge toward the middle. Repeat for the other end of the sash. You should have a 16-inch (40.6 cm) gap of raw edge. Turn the sash right side out, turning the raw edges under, and press it down.

7 Insert ½ inch (1.3 cm) of the apron front and pocket into the gap in the sash. Baste through all layers, making sure the bottom of the sash lines up neatly. Topstitch along the bottom edge of the sash, securing the apron body in place.

josephine

Materials

Apron kit (page 2)

Pattern (page 57)

1 yard (91.4 cm) each of two fabrics — A and B — for the reversible bodice and front bottom

1 yard (90 cm) of a complementary fabric for the neck strap, waistband, ties, and drawstrings

1 yard (90 cm) of muslin

Tear-away stabilizer

Tools

Rotary mat, clear ruler with 45° angle lines, and cutter

Seam ripper

What You Do

1 Enlarge the front bottom template on page 57, and cut it out. Place fabric A, unfolded, on the work surface. Refer to figure 1 to get all the pieces out of 1 yard (90 cm) of material. Pin the front bottom to the fabric, and mark the bodice, casing, and bias strips for the ruffle. Cut out all the pieces. Place fabric B, unfolded, on the work surface and repeat.

2 Place the complementary fabric, folded widthwise, on the work surface and, using the schematic in figure 2, cut out the drawstrings, neck straps, and ties. Cut out the single waistband last, unfolding the fabric to get enough material.

3 To make the neck strap, press ½ inch (1.3 cm) under on each long edge. Fold the strap in half lengthwise and press. Topstitch along each edge.

4 To make the ties, fold each in half lengthwise and press. Open the fold, and press each edge in toward the center. Fold again along the original pressed fold, and topstitch along each edge.

5 Make buttonholes in the bodice casing through which you'll thread the ties. Mark the center point of one casing piece. Using this as a reference, move ¾ inch (1.9 cm)

"The minute I saw the fabric I ended up using for the sashes, the idea of a reversible apron popped into my mind."
— **Valerie Shrader**

down into the fabric to mark the spot to make a ½-inch (1.3 cm) buttonhole. Use the tear-away stabilizer to reinforce the hole as you construct it, following the instructions for your sewing machine. Slice the buttonhole open with the seam ripper. Repeat for the second casing piece.

6 Pin and stitch one bodice casing piece made from fabric A to one bodice piece made of fabric B, with right sides together. Stitch the other casing made out of fabric B to the bodice in fabric A. Trim the seams, and press them toward the bodice.

7 Baste one end of one tie to the wrong side of either casing (figure 3, next page). Don't push the tie through the buttonhole yet. Baste the other tie to the other side. Baste the strap to the same bodice, placing it ⅝ inch (1.6 cm) from the side, with the raw edges even with the raw edges of the casing (figure 4, next page). Be careful not to twist the strap.

8 Pin both bodice pieces together, with right sides together, aligning the seams and matching the center points. Beginning and ending ½ inch (1.3 cm) from the bottom edge, stitch along the sides and top, leaving the entire bottom open, being careful not to catch the ties or straps in the stitching (figure 5, page 29). Trim the seam of the casing only, at the buttonholes, to ⅛ inch (3 mm) to allow the ties to come from either side. Reinforce the stitching at the upper corners of the casing. Turn it right side out.

9 To create the channel for the ties within the casing, pin across the top of the casing, and topstitch close to the edge. Thread the ties through one buttonhole to the right side, and pin in place in the center of the channel. Using a zipper foot if necessary, topstitch along the bottom of the casing as close to the existing seam as possible.

10 Knot the ends of the ties. (When you reverse the apron, untie the knots and slip the ties through the buttonhole on the other

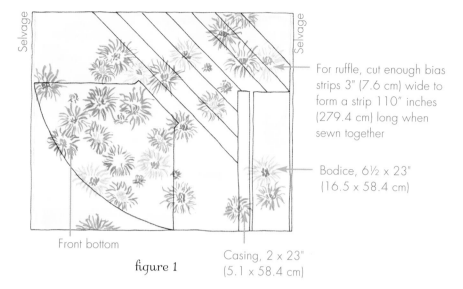

figure 1

For ruffle, cut enough bias strips 3" (7.6 cm) wide to form a strip 110" inches (279.4 cm) long when sewn together

Bodice, 6½ x 23" (16.5 x 58.4 cm)

Front bottom

Casing, 2 x 23" (5.1 x 58.4 cm)

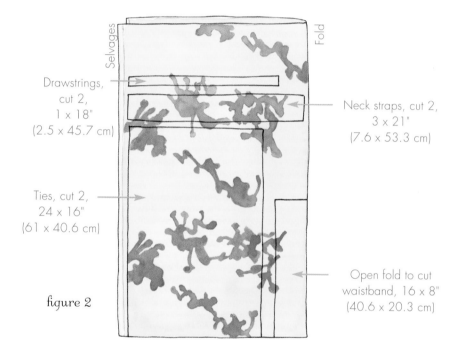

figure 2

Drawstrings, cut 2, 1 x 18" (2.5 x 45.7 cm)

Neck straps, cut 2, 3 x 21" (7.6 x 53.3 cm)

Ties, cut 2, 24 x 16" (61 x 40.6 cm)

Open fold to cut waistband, 16 x 8" (40.6 x 20.3 cm)

"right" side of the casing. Knot them again to secure.)

11 Mark the center points of the bottom edge of the bodice pieces. Gather the bottom edge of the bodice pieces, using long basting stitches.

12 Make the ties and waistband. For the ties, first cut the two 24 x 16-inch (61 x 40.6 cm) tie

pieces in half lengthwise to yield four 24 x 8-inch (61 x 20.3 cm) pieces. Stack and cut them again to yield eight 24 x 4-inch (61 x 10.2 cm) pieces. For the waistband, cut the 16 x 8-inch (40.6 x 20.3 cm) waistband piece in half lengthwise to yield two 16 x 4-inch (40.6 x 10.2 cm) pieces. Mark the center point of each waistband piece. Construct the first waistband/tie with four tie pieces and one waistband piece. Stitch the two tie

figure 3

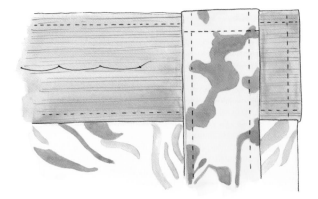

figure 4

pieces together along the short edges, right sides facing. Repeat for the other two pieces. Sew the waistband between these pieces, right sides together, leaving the side seam open ½ inch (1.3 cm) on either side of the bottom of the waistband (the edge that you'll sew to the front bottom). See figure 6. Repeat to make the second waistband/tie, but stitch all the seams completely.

13 Stitch the first waistband/tie piece—the one with the open seam—to the bodice, with the right side together with the fabric A side, along the top of the waistband section only, gathering the bodice to fit and matching side seams and center points. Begin and end the stitching at the ½-inch (1.3 cm) seam left open in step 8 (figure 7). Repeat for the re-

verse side of the waistband/tie and the bodice.

14 With the bodice inside out and the right sides of the waistband/tie together, stitch the long edges and short ends of the ties together, stitching to the ½-inch (1.3 cm) side seam left open on the waistband in step 12 and leaving the front section free. Trim the seams, and turn the waistband/tie right side out. Press it down.

15 Construct a ruffle by cutting strips from fabric A on the bias (figure 1, on page 27) and piecing them to get one strip 110 inches (2.8 m) long. Repeat to construct a second ruffle from fabric B. With the right sides facing, stitch the ruffle pieces together, leaving one long edge open. Trim the seam, turn it right side out, and press it down. Mark the center point of the ruffle.

16 Gather the raw edges of the ruffle using two rows of basting stitches. Pin them to the bottom of one front bottom piece, beginning and ending ½ inch (1.3 cm) from the side edge. Connect the fabric A side of the ruffle to the front bottom of fabric B. With the marks aligned and the raw edges even, baste the ruffle to the front bottom piece. Trim the seam.

17 With the right sides facing, pin and stitch both front bottom pieces together along the sides and hem, leaving the waist open. Begin and end the seam ½ inch (1.3 cm) below the waistline.

18 Pin the fabric A front bottom piece to the same side of the fabric A bodice, right sides facing. Stitch them together.

19 Turn and press under the seam allowance on the remaining waistband/tie. Place it on the ½-inch (1.3 cm) seamline of the fabric B front bottom piece, and slipstitch the opening closed. Decide which pretty side you feel like showing off today, cinch it on, and give a little sashay because you look so good!

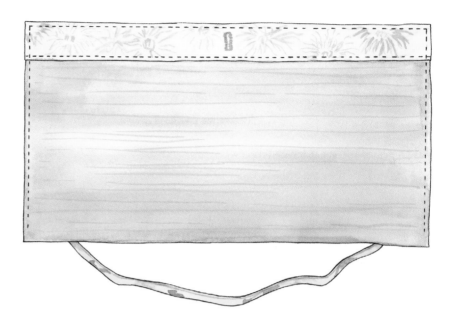

figure 5

figure 6

figure 7

Designer **Carrie Sommer**

psychedelic squares

Materials

Apron kit (page 2)

Pattern (page 58)

1 yard (91.4 cm)
of fabric for the front

½ yard (45.7 cm)
of complementary fabric

Double-fold bias tape

Marking chalk

What You Do

1 Enlarge and cut out the pattern pieces (page 58). Press a crease down the center of the front piece to use in placing the pocket later. Cut a strip of double-fold bias tape a little longer than the top of the pocket.

2 Press the pocket and the pocket binding. Place the top of the pocket between the binding, and pin it.

3 Stitch the binding to the pocket using the left side of the presser foot as a guide. Be sure the binding is sewn on the wrong side as well. Then press the pocket, and snip the excess binding and threads.

4 To make the ties, fold each in half lengthwise, with right sides together and raw edges matching. Press.

5 Stitch the ties with a ¼-inch (6 mm) seam allowance. Pivot ¼ inch (6 mm) from the end, and stitch the end of the tie. Snip the corner of the sewn tie.

6 Turn the tie inside out using a rod or chopstick, and push out the corners. Press the ties flat and even.

7 Finish the ties by topstitching ¼ inch (6 mm) from the sewn edge on two sides.

" I like the fabrics to speak for themselves, so I don't embellish heavily. "
—Carrie Sommer

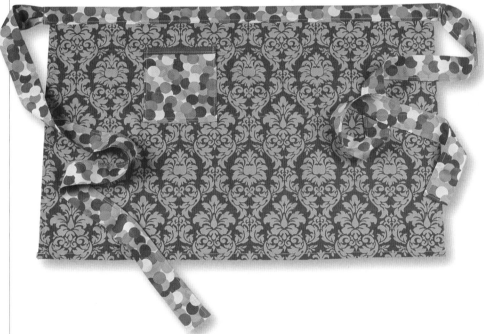

8 To make the front apron piece, start with its sides. Fold in ¼ to ½ inch (6 mm to 1.3 cm) along the edges and press. Fold again to create a double fold, and press again. Pin the folded sides after pressing.

9 Stitch both sides using the left side of your presser foot as a guide. Press again.

10 Determine the top and bottom of the apron then repeat steps 8 and 9 for those edges: with the fabric right side up, double fold, pin, stitch, and press.

11 Turn the fabric right side down, and fold in the sides and bottom ½ inch (1.3 cm). Press.

31

12 Using the center fold as a guide, place the pocket 2 inches (5.1 cm) to the right of the fold and 4½ inches (11.4 cm) down from the top. Pin it in place, and then stitch close to the edge, using the right side of the presser foot as a guide.

13 To make the waistband, turn the cut piece of fabric over so the wrong side is facing up, and fold the ends in 1 inch (2.5 cm). Press the folds.

14 Fold in the cut edge of the fabric ¼ inch (6 mm), and press it. Fold the wrong sides of the fabric together, and press it again.

15 Open, and place the apron front (right side up) flush against the center folded seam (figure 1). Press in place, and pin the two pieces together.

16 Stitch on the waistband using the left side of the presser foot as a guide.

17 To attach the ties, lay the apron out, right side up. Position the ties so the topstitching on each tie lines up with the topstitching of the waistband. Create a pleat with your finger to make the ties the same size as the waistband, and then insert the ties into the folded end of the waistband (figure 2).

18 Stitch along the opening three or four times to create a strong seam. Plan a party: You're going to want to show this one off.

figure 1

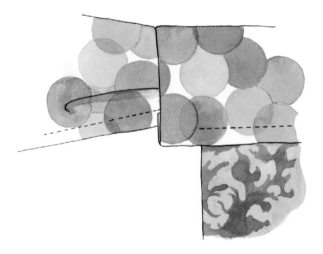

figure 2

mango tango

Materials

Apron kit (page 2)

Pattern (page 59)

1 yard (91.4 cm) of floral fabric

9 yards (8.2 m) of ¼-inch
(6 mm) double-fold bias tape

Tool

Seam leveler

What You Do

1 Make a true bias fold of the fabric, as shown in figure 1. Next, cut the apron pieces, using the pattern on page 59. Transfer the dots on the bottom front pattern onto the fabric. Without pulling or stretching the edges of the pattern pieces, trim all the outer edges to accept the bias tape, and set the pieces aside.

2 If necessary, splice the bias tape together. Save the spliced bias for binding the outer edges of the apron where the splice will be easier to hide.

3 With the right sides together, stitch the two neck strap pieces together at the center back. Press and finish the raw edges to prevent raveling.

4 Attach bias tape to the inner edge of the neck strap. Next, baste the neck strap to the top front, with the wrong sides together.

5 Bind the top edge of the top front (figure 2), including the bottom edges of the neck strap. Press the top front and the neck strap flat.

6 With right sides together and the centers of the pattern pieces aligned, stitch the bottom edge of the top front and tie to the top edge of the bottom front (figure 3).

A good apron becomes like a second skin; you forget you've got it on. If you look flirty in it, well, so much the better!
—Joan Hand Stroh

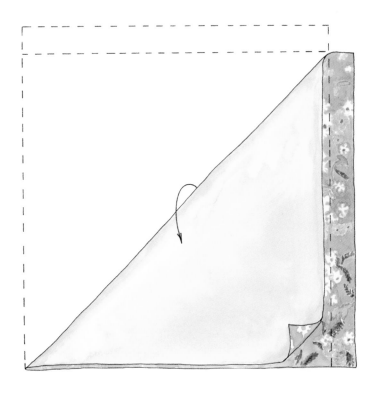

figure 1

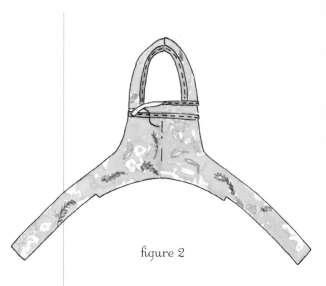

figure 2

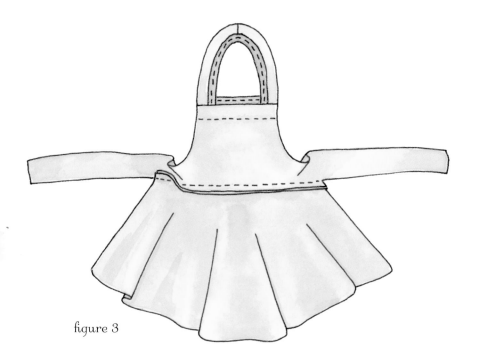

figure 3

7 Trim and bind the edges of the seam. Attach bias tape along the remaining edges of the apron, mitering the corners as needed.

8 Bind the open edge of the pocket, trimming the bias even with the outside edges. Then bind the outer edges of the pocket using a basting stitch and bias tape, mitering the corners.

9 Position the pocket on top of the skirt, matching the corners to the dots on the pattern, and pin it there securely. Fold the pocket edges under approximately ⅜ inch (1 cm). Stitch the pocket in place using a seam leveler at the beginning, end, and corners if necessary. After putting it on, you'll be ready to dance across the kitchen in your new favorite apron.

orange crush

Materials

Apron kit (page 2)

Small amounts of 10 printed fabrics for the patchwork and the towel loop

¾ yard (68.6 cm) of natural-colored linen or cotton for the front

¾ yard (68.6 cm) of muslin for the lining

¼ yard (22.9 cm) of floral print for the pocket

¾ yard (68.6 cm) of gingham for the waistband and ties

6 inches (15.2 cm) of lace for the pocket

¾ yard (68.6 cm) each of three different laces, in varying widths but at least ½ inch (1.3 cm) wide for the patchwork

Tools

Rotary cutter and mat (optional)

Seam allowance:

¼ inch (6 mm)

unless otherwise noted

What You Do

1 Cut all the pieces you'll need using the schematic (figure 1, next page) as your guide. You'll cut the lace later as described in subsequent steps.

2 To make the pocket, use the 6-inch (15.2 cm) piece of lace. Lay the larger pocket-lining piece right side up. Lay the lace on top of it, wrong side up, and then the smaller pocket front, also wrong side up, matching the top edges. Pin and then sew them all together. Press the seam toward the larger pocket piece.

3 Match the bottom edge of the pocket front end to end with the pocket lining, right sides together. Press it flat. Turn both bottom edges ¼ inch (6 mm) toward the wrong side, and press it again. Pin the pocket together along the sides, and then sew up the sides. Turn it right side out, and press it again.

4 Pin the pocket to the apron front 4½ inches (11.4 cm) from the side edge and 6 inches (15.2 cm) from the top edge. Sew it in place by topstitching ⅛ inch (3 mm) along the pocket sides and bottom.

5 To make the towel loop, fold the 4 x 7-inch (10.2 x 17.8 cm) rectangle in half lengthwise, wrong sides together, and press. Open it, bring in

"Patchwork strips and delicate lace give this apron a vintage, old-fashioned charm, while the graphic prints and simple lines look contemporary."
—Erin Harris

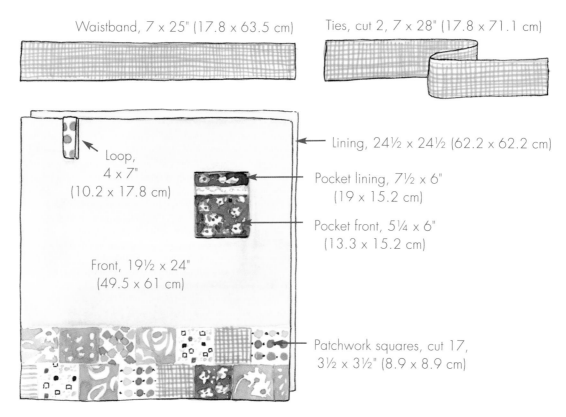

Waistband, 7 x 25" (17.8 x 63.5 cm)

Ties, cut 2, 7 x 28" (17.8 x 71.1 cm)

Loop,
4 x 7"
(10.2 x 17.8 cm)

Lining, 24½ x 24½ (62.2 x 62.2 cm)

Pocket lining, 7½ x 6"
(19 x 15.2 cm)

Pocket front, 5¼ x 6"
(13.3 x 15.2 cm)

Front, 19½ x 24"
(49.5 x 61 cm)

Patchwork squares, cut 17,
3½ x 3½" (8.9 x 8.9 cm)

figure 1

the side edges toward the middle fold, and press again. Fold it in half again, and press once more. Pin it together along its open side, and topstitch ⅛ inch (3 mm) from each side edge. Line up both raw edges with the top edge of the apron, 3 inches (7.6 cm) in from the side. Sew it in place ¼ inch (6 mm) from the top edge.

6 Assemble the patchwork squares into two strips: one eight squares long and one nine squares long. Sew them together, and press the seams open.

7 Pin a length of the lace to the top edge of the longer patchwork piece, right side up, and baste it in place ⅛ inch (3 mm) from the edge. Trim away any extra lace. Pin the patchwork strips right sides together, centering the shorter piece like brickwork above the longer piece so the seams don't line up (figure 2). Sew the strips together. Press the seam toward the shorter strip and the lace toward the longer strip. Trim the edges of the longer patchwork strip, so it's even with the shorter one (figure 3).

8 Pin the second length of lace to the top edge of the patchwork, right side up, and baste it in place ⅛ inch (3 mm) from the edge. Trim away any extra lace. Pin the patchwork strip to the apron front, right sides together, and sew it using a ¼-inch (6 mm) seam. Press the seam toward the apron front and the lace toward the patchwork.

9 Cut a piece of lace 24½ inches (62.2 cm) long. Hem the edges by turning ⅛ inch (3 mm) toward the wrong side, and then turning ⅛ inch (3 mm) again, and stitching in place. Pin it to the bottom edge of the patch-

work, right sides together, lining up raw edges, starting and ending ¼ inch (6 mm) in from the ends. Baste it in place ⅛ inch (3 mm) from the edge.

10 To make the ties, fold each rectangle in half lengthwise with right sides together to form two 3½ x 28-inch (8.9 x 71.1 cm) pieces. Press them, and then sew each long side with a ½-inch (1.3 cm) seam. On one open end, sew a ½-inch (1.3 cm) seam. Clip the corners, and trim the seams to ¼ inch (6 mm). Turn each tie right side out, and press it again. Topstitch the three closed sides of each tie ⅛ inch (3 mm) from the edge.

11 Pin the apron front to the lining, right sides together, and sew ¼-inch (6 mm) seams along the sides and the bottom, being careful not to catch the lace in the side seams. Turn it right side out and press. Sew the lining to the front ¼ inch (6 mm) from the top edge.

12 Fold each end of the waistband in ½ inch (1.3 cm) and press. Then fold the waistband in half lengthwise, wrong sides together, and press. Open the waistband, and fold one raw edge ½ inch (1.3 cm) toward the wrong side, and press it in place.

13 Pin the apron front to the front of the waistband, right sides together, matching the edges. Sew a ½-inch (1.3 cm) seam. Press the seam toward the waistband. With the wrong side of the apron facing up, flip the waistband down, covering the seam, and pin it in place. On the right side, stitch the waistband ⅛ inch (3 mm) from the seam, catching the back of the waistband at the same time. Topstitch ⅛ inch (3 mm) from the edge along the top of the waistband.

14 To attach the ties, insert the raw edge of each tie about ½ inch (1.3 cm) into the waistband opening on each side. Stitch in place ⅛ inch (3 mm) from the waistband edge.

figure 2

figure 3

twirl, girl!

Materials

Apron kit (page 2)

Pattern (page 56)

1 yard (91.4 cm) of cotton fabric in a solid color

1 yard (91.4 cm) of printed cotton fabric

Tools

Quilters mat (optional)

Sewing gauge

What You Do

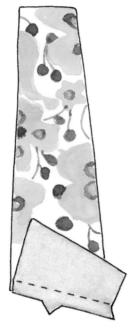

figure 1

1 Using the pattern on page 56, cut out the fabric pieces.

2 Pin one hem piece to the bottom of a front piece, right sides together and matching the notch (figure 1). Stitch a seam along the edge. Press the seams toward the hem, and topstitch close to the seam. Repeat, attaching each hem piece to a front piece.

3 Lay out one panel, right side up, and place another panel on top of it, right side down, with the edges matching. The top edge of both panels should line up as well. Pin and sew a seam along the edge. Repeat this step, connecting all the panels together. At the hem, the bottom panels should meet like the teeth of a saw

(figure 2, next page). Press the seams open, then press them all to the same side. Topstitch all the seams.

4 Make ¼-inch (6 mm) hems on both sides and at the bottom.

5 Make the waistband from the solid fabric, cutting a piece 7 x 22 inches (17.8 x 55.9 cm). Fold the waistband in half crosswise to find the center line, and mark a crease by ironing it. Find the center line of the apron, and mark it the same way.

6 Place the waistband on top of the apron front, right sides together, and line up the top edges at the crease marks. Pin. Stitch a seam along the raw edges, attaching the waistband to the front. (The extra fabric at the edges is for the seam allowances for the apron ties.)

7 Turn the apron front and waistband over, and fold the long edge of the waistband ½ inch (1.3 cm) in toward the wrong side. Press it down. Fold the waistband in half, matching up the long folded edge to the edge attached to the apron, and iron a crease.

8 To make the ties, cut two pieces of solid fabric, each 6 x 37 inches (15.2 x 94 cm). Fold each tie in half lengthwise with the right sides together and pin. Stitch a seam along

the edge and one end of each tie. Trim off the seam allowances, turn the ties right side out, and press. Topstitch the edges.

9 Place the apron front and waist-band right side up on your work surface. Pin one tie to one side of the waistband, matching the raw edges, close to the seam holding the front to the waistband. Repeat, pinning the other tie to the other side of the waistband.

10 Fold the waistband in half along the crease, right sides together, over the ties (figure 3). Make sure the waistband edges meet. Stitch a seam along the raw edges of the ties and waistband, sewing it in a straight line up along the sides of the waistband. Trim off the seam allowances, and turn the waistband right side out by pulling on both the apron ties.

11 With the apron facing right side down, pin the bottom of the waistband down to the seam holding the waistband to the front of the apron. Stitch a ¼-inch (6 mm) seam along the bottom edge of the waist-band. Give it a final press, put it on, and twirl. It's time for a cocktail!

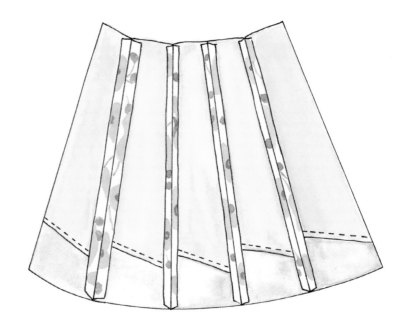

figure 2

figure 3

Designer Joan K. Morris

Summertime blues

Materials

Apron kit (page 2)

Pattern (pages 60–61)

1 yard (91.4 cm) of floral fabric for the apron front, sides, and bodice

¾ yard (68.6 cm) of complementary fabric for the lower hem, waistband, waist ties, neck ties, and bodice edging

½ yard (45.7 cm) of striped fabric for the upper hem

1½ yards (1.4 m) of gathered lace trim

Seam allowance:
¼ inch (6 mm)
unless otherwise noted

What You Do

1 Use the pattern (pages 60 and 61) to cut out the apron pieces. From the floral fabric, cut out the bodice (2), the waistband lining (1), and the apron front (1), and sides (2). From the complementary fabric, cut out the neck ties (2), the bodice lining (2), the waistband (1), the waist ties (2), and the lower hem front (1), and sides (2). From the striped fabric, cut out the upper hem front (1) and the sides (2).

2 Pin and stitch each bodice edging piece to each bodice. Clip the curves and press. With the right sides together, stitch the two bodice pieces together at the front center, matching the notches and creating a seam there.

3 Fold each neck tie in half lengthwise with the wrong sides together. Stitch each together, leaving one end open. Trim the seam and the corners.

4 Turn the neck ties right side out and press. Topstitch them close to the seamed edges. Baste each tie to a bodice edging.

5 With the right sides together, stitch the two bodice lining pieces to the bodice pieces—over the neck ties—leaving the lower edges open. Reinforce the stitching at the center front seam, being careful not to catch the neck tie in the stitching. Trim the seam, and clip the curves.

6 Turn the bodice right side out and press, flattening the neck ties. Baste the raw lower edges together. Gather the lower edge between the notches, stitching through all thicknesses.

7 With the right sides together, pin the lower edge of the bodice to the upper edge of the waistband, matching the notches. Make sure the raw edges are even. Pull up the gathering stitches to fit, and then baste (figure 1). Set aside.

8 Take the waistband lining, and machine stitch ⅝ inch (1.6 cm) along its lower edge. Press under the edge along the stitching (figure 2). Place the element made in step 7 on your work surface, laying it out as shown in figure 1. Pin the waistband lining to it, with the right sides together, referring to figure 2. Stitch a seam through all the thicknesses. Trim the seam, clip the curves, and press the waistband and lining from the back, pressing the seam toward the waistband.

9 Machine stitch the apron front to the upper hem front, with a ⅝-inch (1.6 cm) seam allowance and right sides together. Also stitch the apron sides to the upper hem sides. Press all the seams open. Hem the edges.

10 Fold the top and bottom edges of the lower hem (front and sides) in ¼ inch (6 mm). Press. Place the lace trim under the lower edge of the upper hem with the ruffle out. Pin the lace and the front and sides of the lower hem in place. Machine stitch the edge of the lower hem front and sides on the seam line, catching the trim as well.

11 Stitch the apron front to the sides, matching the upper and lower hem seams.

12 With the right sides together, pin the apron front and sides to the lower edge of the waistband,

figure 1

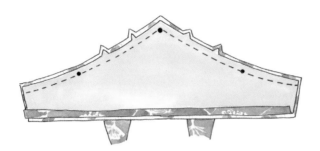

figure 2

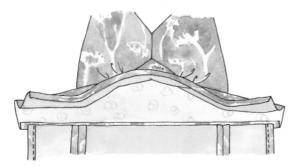

figure 3

matching the center point and notches (figure 3). Stitch the seam, and then trim it. Clip the curves. Press the seam toward the waistband.

13 Fold the ties in half lengthwise, with the right sides together. Stitch the seam, leaving one end open. Trim the seam and the corners.

14 Turn the ties right side out and press. Topstitch close to the seamed edges. On the outside, pin the open end of each tie to the edge of the waistband, one on each side. Baste them together.

15 Fold the waistband with the right sides together—over the ties—and stitch across the ends through all thicknesses. Trim the seam and the corners.

16 Turn the waistband right side out. On the inside, pin the pressed edge of the waistband facing over the seam, placing the pins on the outside. On the outside, stitch the waistband close to all the seams, catching in the pressed edge of the facing on the underside. Tie it on, invite a friend over for lemonade, and bask in the compliments.

kaleidoscope

Materials

Apron kit (page 2)

Pattern (page 62)

¾ yard (68.6 cm) of fabric for the front

¾ yard (68.6 cm) of coordinating fabric for the waistband, hem, and ties

¼ yard (22.9 cm) of batiste for the waistband lining

4 buttons (with holes, not shanks), ⅞-inch (2.2 cm) in diameter

Tools

Spaghetti-strap turner

Seam gauge

What You Do

1 Enlarge and cut out the pattern pieces on page 62. Cut the front out of the main fabric and the remaining pattern pieces out of the coordinating fabric. Cut the waistband out of the batiste.

2 Overlock, serge, or zigzag all the raw edges of the front and hem pieces to prevent them from fraying.

3 With right sides together, pin the hem to the front, starting from the center and working toward the edges to ensure the edges match up correctly. Stitch.

4 Press the seam toward the hem, and then topstitch the seam down on the right side of the fabric.

5 Turn to the wrong side. Press and stitch down the sides.

6 Turn back to the right side, press the hem, and stitch it down.

7 Turn the four tie pieces over, wrong side up, and press one end of each, so the right side is turned over to the wrong side.

I used pin-tucks to confer the formality of an obi or a corset. It was exciting to discover their value as both a structural and a textural element.

—Angelina Williamson

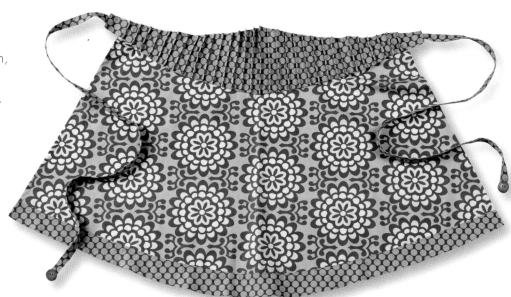

8 Pin two ties together, right sides together, and stitch the sides using a ¼-inch (6 mm) seam allowance. Repeat to create the other tie.

9 Turn the ties right side out using the spaghetti-strap turner, and press them. Topstitch three sides, leaving the raw edge unstitched.

10 With the right sides together, pin the waistband to the waistband lining. Stitch the sides, using a ¼-inch (6 mm) seam allowance. Turn the waistband right side out and press.

11 Turn in the ends of the waistband ½ inch (1.3 cm) and press. Insert the raw end of each apron strap into the ends of the waistband. Pin them in place, and topstitch the entire waistband.

12 Use a temporary-ink fabric pen to mark the center of the waistband at the top and the bottom. On one side of the center, use the seam gauge to make 15 small marks at the top and the bottom edges of the waistband at 1¼-inch (3.2 cm) intervals, starting from the center and working your way out. Repeat on the other side of the center mark.

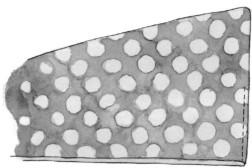

figure 1

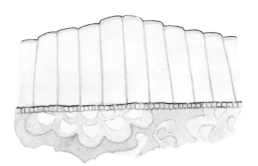

figure 2

13 Fold the waistband at the center, wrong sides together. Stitch a seam ¼ inch (6 mm) in from the center fold. Work from the center out toward one end (figure 1), and then turn the waistband around, and repeat to finish the other end. Refer to the marks you made to fold each tuck at the right spot. Stitch ¼ inch (6 mm) in from the fold each time.

14 Using a temporary-ink fabric pen, mark the center of the waistband by measuring its longest vertical length and dividing that number in half. Pin the front of the apron to the point you've marked. Then pin the rest of the front to the waistband, keeping it centered along the waistband (figure 2).

15 Use an uneven slipstitch to sew the apron front to the waistband.

16 Sandwich the end of each apron tie between two buttons, and stitch the buttons to each other. Put it on and go out for ice cream. You'll look as cool as you feel.

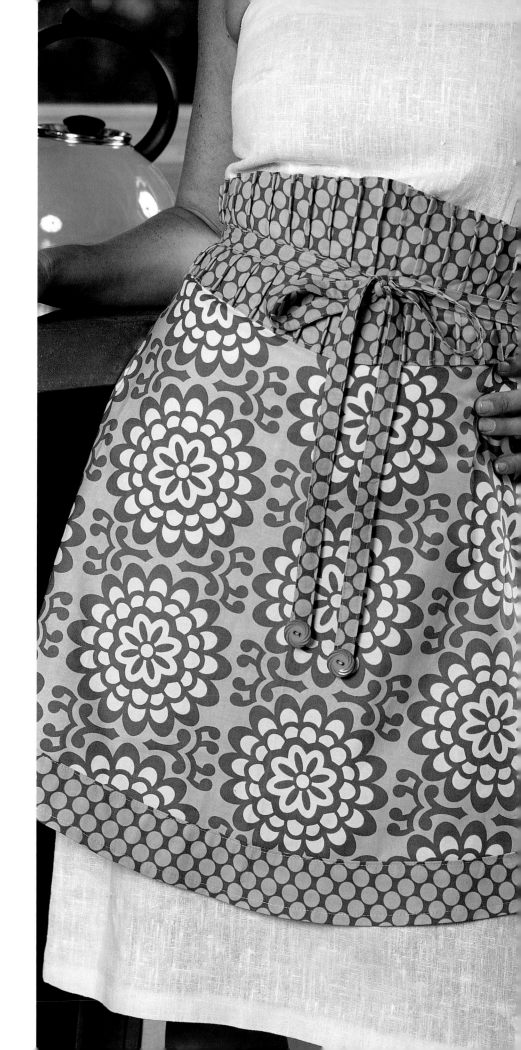

Designer Nathalie Mornu

skirt the issue

What You Need

Apron kit (page 2)

An old skirt

9 inches (22.9 cm) of complementary fabric

How You Make It

1 Cut the skirt along the side seams and retain the front half. Hem both sides of it. Hem the bottom shorter if you wish.

2 Cut the complementary fabric into three strips lengthwise, so that you end up with three bands 3 inches (7.6 cm) wide.

3 Sew two of the bands together along the short edge, right sides together. Use this strip to make a waistband for the apron.

4 Cut the remaining band of complementary fabric in half down its length. Stitch both pieces together along the short edge, with right sides together. Sew basting stitches down the center, and gather evenly and tightly to make a ruffle. Pin the ruffle to the bottom above the hemline; topstitch along the center of the ruffle to attach it to the apron.

Templates

Amoeba, page 9
Enlarge 400%

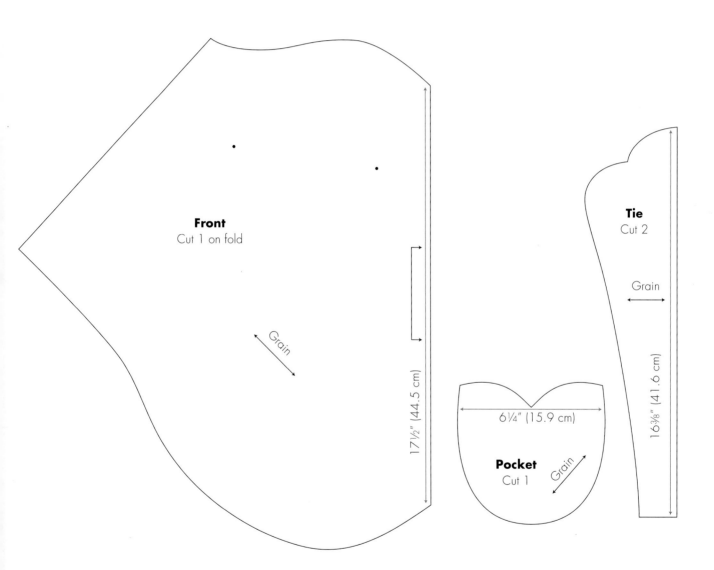

Front
Cut 1 on fold

Grain

17½" (44.5 cm)

6¼" (15.9 cm)

Pocket
Cut 1

Grain

Tie
Cut 2

Grain

16⅜" (41.6 cm)

Cakeland, page 12

Enlarge 400%

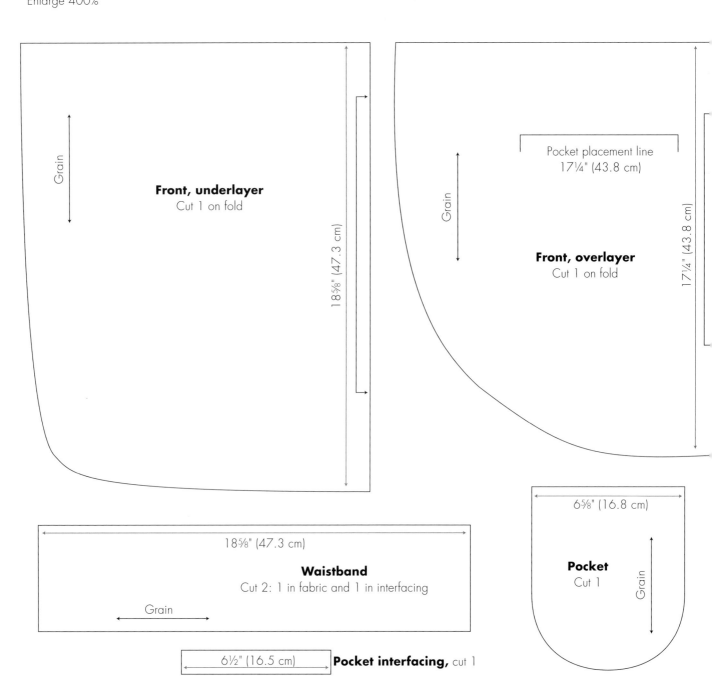

Front, underlayer
Cut 1 on fold

Grain

18⅝" (47.3 cm)

Pocket placement line
17¼" (43.8 cm)

Front, overlayer
Cut 1 on fold

Grain

17¼" (43.8 cm)

18⅝" (47.3 cm)

Waistband
Cut 2: 1 in fabric and 1 in interfacing

Grain

6⅝" (16.8 cm)

Pocket
Cut 1

Grain

6½" (16.5 cm) **Pocket interfacing,** cut 1

Cherry Bistro, page 14

Enlarge 600%

Grain

Tie
Cut 2

6¼" (15.9 cm)

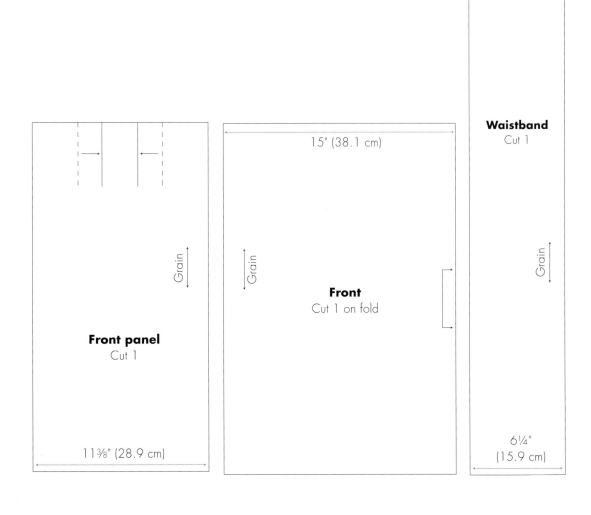

Waistband
Cut 1

15" (38.1 cm)

Grain

Grain

Grain

Front
Cut 1 on fold

Front panel
Cut 1

11⅜" (28.9 cm)

6¼"
(15.9 cm)

Lemon Meringue, page 16
Enlarge 400%

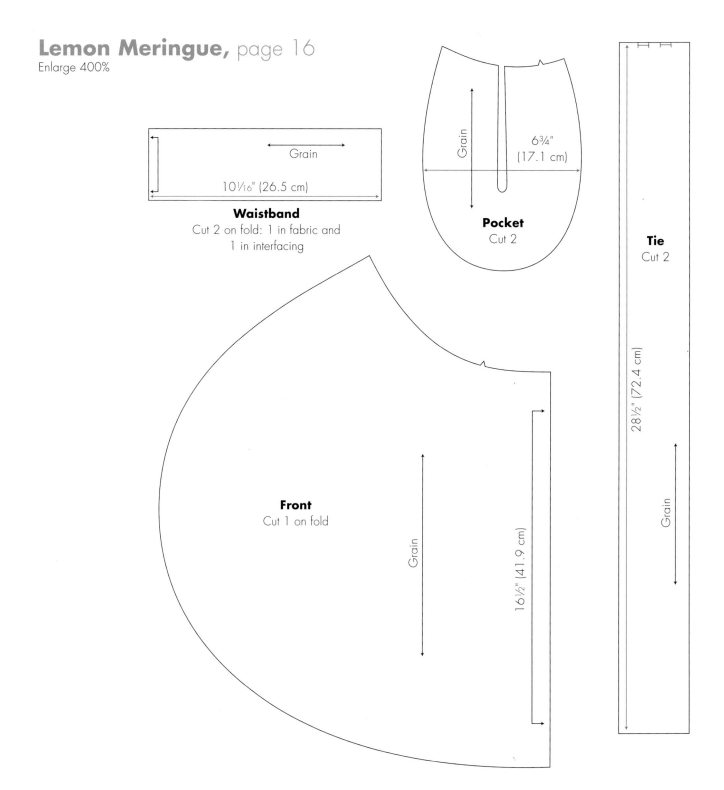

Waistband
Cut 2 on fold: 1 in fabric and
1 in interfacing

Grain

10¹⁄₁₆" (26.5 cm)

Pocket
Cut 2

Grain

6¾"
(17.1 cm)

Tie
Cut 2

28½" (72.4 cm)

Grain

Front
Cut 1 on fold

Grain

16½" (41.9 cm)

Fruit Tart, page 19

Enlarge 400%

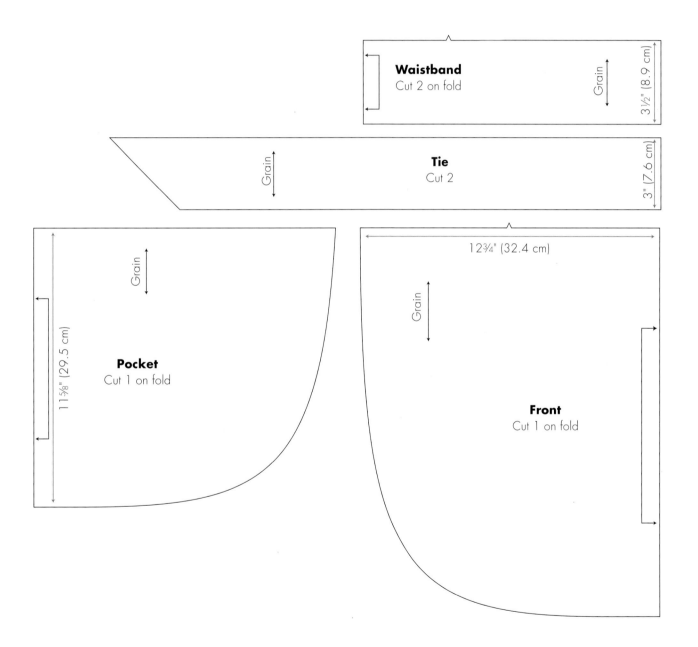

Waistband
Cut 2 on fold

Grain

3½" (8.9 cm)

Tie
Cut 2

Grain

3" (7.6 cm)

Pocket
Cut 1 on fold

Grain

11⅝" (29.5 cm)

12¾" (32.4 cm)

Grain

Front
Cut 1 on fold

Deep Pockets, page 22
Enlarge 400%

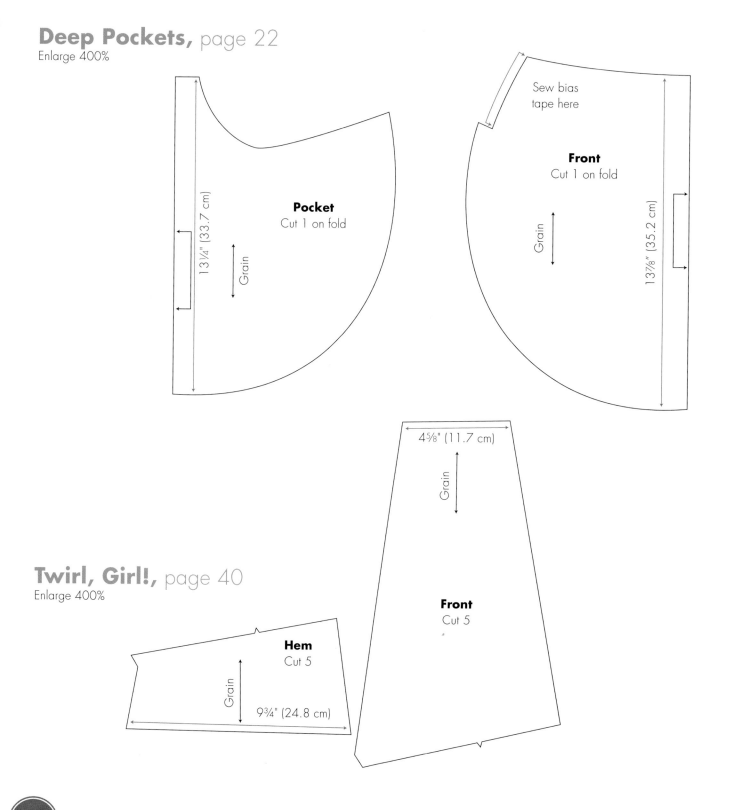

Pocket
Cut 1 on fold

13¼" (33.7 cm)

Grain

Sew bias
tape here

Front
Cut 1 on fold

Grain

13⅞" (35.2 cm)

4⅝" (11.7 cm)

Grain

Front
Cut 5

Twirl, Girl!, page 40
Enlarge 400%

Hem
Cut 5

Grain

9¾" (24.8 cm)

Josephine, page 25
Enlarge 400%

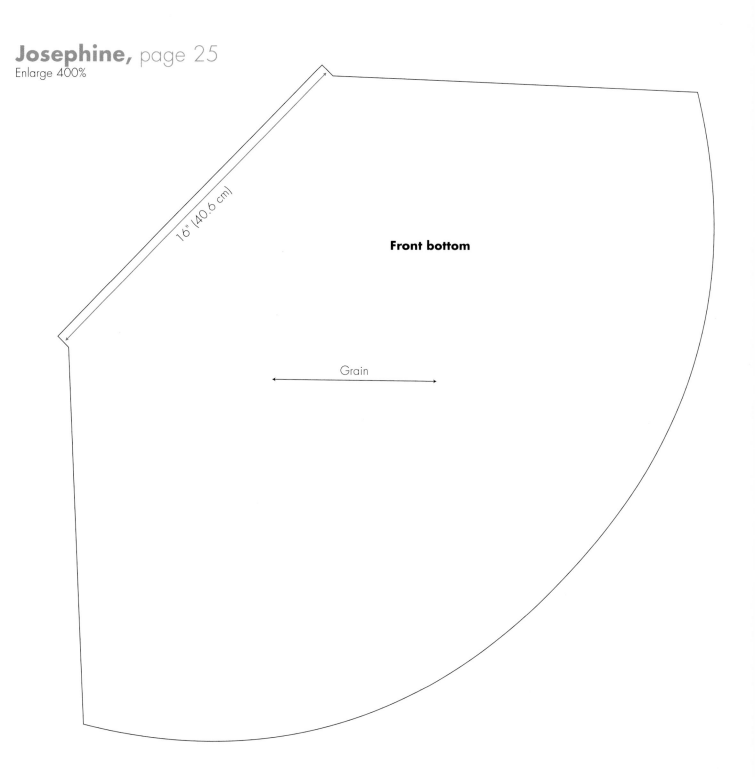

16" (40.6 cm)

Front bottom

Grain

Psychedelic Squares, page 30
Enlarge 500%

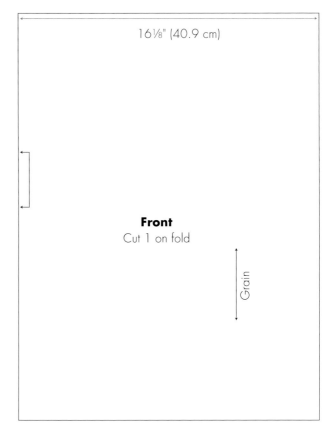

16⅛" (40.9 cm)

Front
Cut 1 on fold

Grain

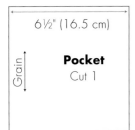

6½" (16.5 cm)

Grain

Pocket
Cut 1

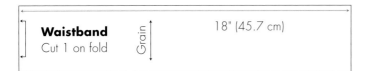

Waistband
Cut 1 on fold

Grain

18" (45.7 cm)

36" (91.4 cm)

Grain

Tie
Cut 2

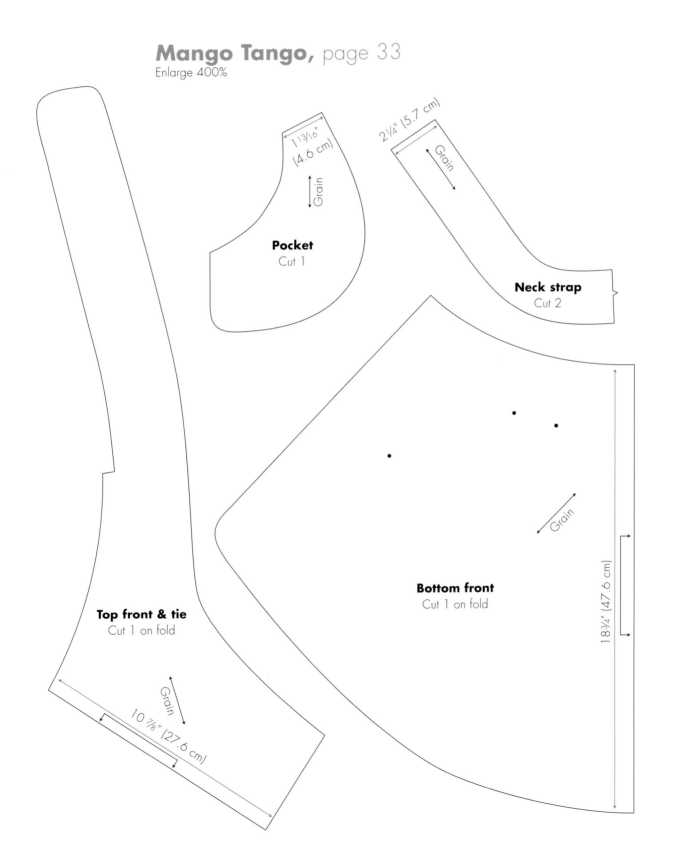

Mango Tango, page 33

Enlarge 400%

1 13/16" (4.6 cm)

Grain

Pocket
Cut 1

2¼" (5.7 cm)

Grain

Neck strap
Cut 2

Bottom front
Cut 1 on fold

Grain

18¾" (47.6 cm)

Top front & tie
Cut 1 on fold

Grain

10 7⁄8" (27.6 cm)

Summertime Blues, page 43

Enlarge 400%

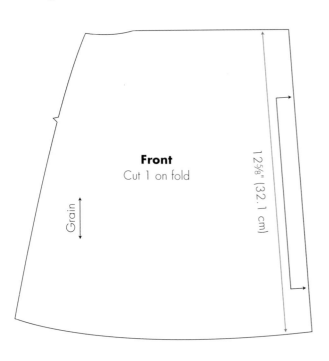

Front
Cut 1 on fold

Grain

12⅝" (32.1 cm)

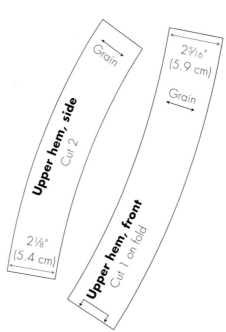

Upper hem, side
Cut 2

Grain

2⅛"
(5.4 cm)

2⁵⁄₁₆"
(5.9 cm)

Grain

Upper hem, front
Cut 1 on fold

3¼" (8.3 cm)

Grain

Neck tie
Cut 2

Tie
Cut 2

27¾" (70.5 cm)

Grain

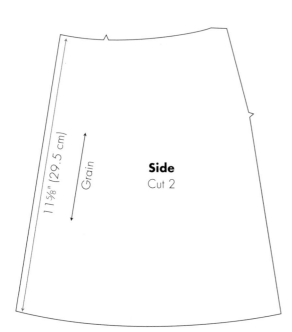

11⅝" (29.5 cm)

Grain

Side
Cut 2